For Good Luck!

by Katrina Gold
Illustrated by Wednesday Kirwan

PEARSON
Scott Foresman

Editorial Offices: Glenview, Illinois • Parsippany, New Jersey • New York, New York
Sales Offices: Needham, Massachusetts • Duluth, Georgia • Glenview, Illinois
Coppell, Texas • Sacramento, California • Mesa, Arizona

Lyn and her brother David had to stay inside because it was raining. Mom had an idea. "Let's look into the memory box!"

Mom used that box to keep special things, her treasures. She said those treasures helped her remember things that happened in the past.

---

treasures: valuable things

The children remembered the memory box. They loved it. The memory box had many things: David's first baby tooth, Lyn's old first tiny pair of shoes with red shoelaces, and old photographs. Mostly, they liked the stories Mom told them about the treasures in the box.

Mom unpacked the memory box. She took the treasures out of the box one at a time. Lyn was curious about a small case. David found a small cloth bag.

---

case: a box to hold something

Lyn asked, "Mom, is this case for the earrings?" "Yes," answered Mom as she touched her earrings. She had a strange smile on her face. "Tell us the story about them again," begged Lyn. Mom answered, "You know that the earrings are these rings I am wearing on my ears now."

"This is the story of my lucky earrings," Mom said. "These earrings belonged to my mother—your Grandma Liu. My father gave them to her when they got married in China. He said that the earrings would protect her and give her luck. She wore those earrings every day, and she was very lucky!"

"When I left China to come to the United States, Grandma Liu gave the earrings to me. Lyn, some day, I will give them to you." David frowned, but Lyn smiled.

David asked about the cloth bag. Mom opened it and took out a wrapped thing. She opened it. It was a piece of jade. "David, Grandpa found this stone by the mountains in China and carried it in his pocket every day! It will be yours one day." Now David smiled.

Do you have a treasure?

---

jade: hard green stone